RAPHA

God My Healer

Heal me, O Lord and I will be healed...
Jeremiah 17:14 (NKJ)

Written by: W. Wilkinson III
Character Illustrations by: talywa
Background Illustrations by: Alyssa Baker

To My Little Angel <u>Noah Prince</u>

With LOVE from <u>Grand Dad & Nana Ro</u>

Date <u>April</u> / <u>20</u> / <u>2015</u>

Pray always baby, your words are
Powerful like lightening!

We love you very much.

THE NAMES OF THE ANGELS OF AGAPE CHARACTERS ARE BASED ON THE DIFFERENT NAMES OF GOD AND THEIR MEANINGS ARE TAKEN FROM SCRIPTURE. WE HAVE REMOVED THE PREFIXES "EL" AND "JEHOVAH" FROM THE NAMES LEAVING ONLY THE ADJECTIVE TO MAKE THE NAMES EASIER FOR CHILDREN TO LEARN AND UNDERSTAND. FURTHERMORE, CALLING ANY ENTITY OTHER THAN GOD BY THE FULL NAME OF EL... OR JEHOVAH... WOULD GO AGAINST OUR BELIEFS. MOST OF ALL WE WANT TO REINFORCE OUR MESSAGE THAT THERE IS ONLY ONE TRUE AND LIVING GOD.

Dedication

This book is dedicated to my son, Noah, who was rushed to the hospital while in acute kidney failure and underwent surgery on Christmas Eve 2012. By God's amazing grace his kidney function is steadily improving as we are expecting God to continue to heal and restore him to 100%; in the matchless name of Jesus. Amen!

Special thanks to all of the family members and friends who have and continue to pray for Noah in addition to the doctors, nurses and staff at Pocono Medical Center's Emergency Room and at the Janet Weis Children's Hospital - Geisinger Health System in Danville, PA, as well as the doctors who continue to care for and monitor him.

There once was a child who looked just like you,
Same age, same eyes, and smiled like you too.
The child was sick and felt really bad,
Not being able to play made the little one sad.

"Why me Lord?" The child said in sorrow.
"Is there something that I did to deserve to feel awful?
What can I do, where should I begin,
To make everything better and feel good again?"

God sent a messenger when He heard the little one's prayer.
Rapha was the angel who carried the message there.
For he is the angel God sends down from heaven
To teach and remind us of the blessings God has given.

Quickly Rapha flew,
Just as God told him to.
In an instant he was there,
With the message he had to share.

When Rapha arrived, the child was in bed.

"Hi my name is Rapha." The guardian angel said.

"I am one of the messengers who delivers the Word of God."

The child didn't say a word, instead just gave a nod.

Rapha reached into his backpack to get his golden tablet,

It contained the Word of God and His message written on it.

From the moment Rapha landed he had a mission to fulfill,

To deliver God's words of healing, to the child that was ill.

"God is a healer!" Rapha stated boldly.

"Here's the message that I have, this is what God told me.

You didn't do anything wrong, so don't worry your little head.

You are very special in God's eyes." Rapha smiled and said.

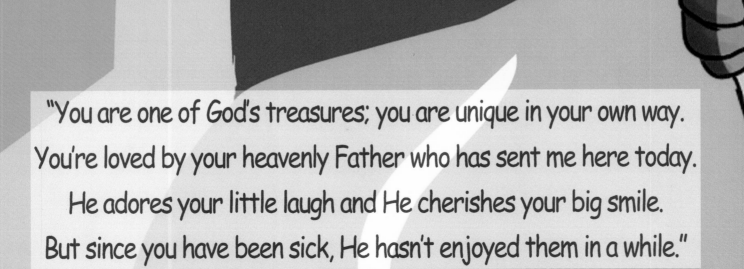

"You are one of God's treasures; you are unique in your own way.

You're loved by your heavenly Father who has sent me here today.

He adores your little laugh and He cherishes your big smile.

But since you have been sick, He hasn't enjoyed them in a while."

"He loves seeing you play and it brings Him such joy.

Whether you play a game, or play outside or with your favorite toy.

He also loves the very things that you love and like to do.

He made them all for you to enjoy, just as He made you."

"Remember what makes you happy and makes you feel good inside.
Think about what makes you laugh with a smile you cannot hide.
Dream about the special things that you hold dear to your heart.
This will help you feel better and is a good place for you to start."

"You'll need to draw on your inner strength to help you to get through.
And call on the power of God who will give that strength to you.
Don't ever be ashamed to trust the mighty name of Jesus.
He is our Savior, He has the power to comfort and to heal us."

"Big hurts, little hurts and everything in between,
Hurts of the heart and of the body, both seen and unseen.
First you need to talk to God and tell Him what's on your mind.
Just start by saying hello to Him and the rest will come in time."

"Tell God what makes you sad so you can smile with joy again.
Tell Him all the fears you have and He'll restore your light within.
God wants to hear from you, so don't be afraid to let Him know
Just what it is you need from Him and how you need Him so."

"Take joy in knowing you have a friend in Him who loves you dear.
Know that you can talk to God at anytime and anywhere.
There will be times when you don't feel as well as you did before.
It will take a while before you fly but soon you'll learn to soar."

The child looked at Rapha and said with a smile,
"I think I know just what to do, it was in me all the while."
The child's head was bowed and eyes were closed so tight.
The child said this prayer of healing with sincerity and might.

"Dear Lord," the little child said...
"Thank You for the love
that I have come to know.
Please touch and heal my body
from my head down to my toe.
Thank You Lord for taking time
and answering my prayer.
And Thank You Lord for sending
Your angel Rapha here.
AMEN.

VISIT ANGELSOFAGAPE.COM FOR A SELECTION OF CHILDREN'S PRAYERS, DEVOTIONS AND AFFIRMATIONS FOR YOU AND YOUR LITTLE ANGEL(S) TO ENJOY TOGETHER.

ANGELS OF AGAPE
PUBLISHING

FEATURING

FOR OTHER BOOKS YOU AND YOUR ANGEL(S) WILL ENJOY, VISIT ANGELSOFAGAPE.COM

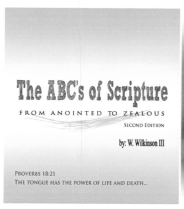

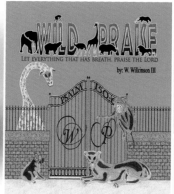
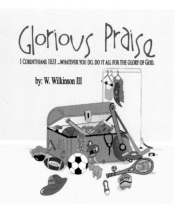

ABC's of Scripture   Traci's Praise   Wild Praise   Glorious Praise

JOIN, FOLLOW AND SHARE US ON FACEBOOK AT:
CHRISTIAN CHILDREN'S BOOKS BY ANGELS OF AGAPE
AND OUR FACEBOOK GROUP FOR PRAYERS OF HEALING:
RAPHA: GOD MY HEALER

FROM YOUR FRIENDS AT ANGELS OF AGAPE PUBLISHING AND NOAH... GOD BLESS.

CPSIA information can be obtained
at www.ICGtesting.com
Printed in the USA
BVIC01n0035070214
344221BV00002B/3

* 9 7 8 1 6 3 0 6 8 0 0 3 9 *